Love,
Barley

With deep respect for all
creatures great and small.

Gail Diederich   Lila Murray

BARLEY

A Possum's Own Story

Written by Gail Diederich
With Lea Murray

the Peppertree Press

Sarasota, Florida

For information regarding permission,
call 941-922-2662 or contact us at our website:
www.peppertreepublishing.com or write to:
the Peppertree Press, LLC.
Attention: Publisher
1269 First Street, Suite 7
Sarasota, Florida 34236

ISBN: 978-1-61493-275-8

Library of Congress Number: 2014908507

Printed in the U.S.A.

Printed July 2014

Acknowledgements

Sincere thanks to Rene VanHout of LOL Transport and Moving, Lutz, Florida, for her generous support and encouragement with the publication of this book.

We extend appreciation to Barley's friends who have freely shared their pictures of him. It's impossible to recognize everyone by name, but our heartfelt thanks to those who have come to love Barley, enjoy snapping pictures of him at various events and post them to Facebook for all to enjoy. Those efforts help promote the knowledge of this wonderful little fellow and possums in general.

Dedication

This book is dedicated with appreciation to my friend Ardis Christensen Padgett for her encouragement and support and especially for her assistance with editing; to my husband, Jay Diederich, for his unending patience and love and for his skills as "the grammar police"; to teaching colleague and friend Shine Stevens for reading and contributing helpful suggestions; to my longtime friend Linda Young for her encouragement and unending words of support. My deepest appreciation to Barley and Lea Murray for inviting me into their lives to write their story so that others may come to change an attitude about possums, as I have, and to realize once again how fortunate we all are to live in a world filled with incredible animals and how much learning they offer to all of us. Finally, my writing is always for our grandchildren – Alysia Diederich, Meaghan and Finn Schlossmacher; Avery, Adelle and Ruby Kenney and Josephine, Lucy and Maverick Bazin. May these wonderful children always love reading!

— Gail Diederich

It was a treasured moment when Barley and Gail
put the finishing touches on this special book.

Dedication

With so much appreciation, Barley and I dedicate this book to the unnamed woman who cared enough to stop on the highway, gather up and bring an injured possum family for veterinary help on a dark, chilly March night. Without that beginning, none of this would have been possible. Our extreme gratitude to all of Barley's Facebook "friends" for the sincere love and support they have for Barley and possums in general; to his amazing doctors, Dr. Linda Register and Dr. Michele Farrar for their dedication in giving him the best veterinary care possible; to Jade Sceusa for all her love and hard work in organizing birthday and Christmas parties to help raise awareness and money for our cause and to Gail Diederich for her amazing talents and commitment that brought so much of this to life. We thank all the possum rehabilitators, forever home caregivers, and good Samaritans that nurture and care for possums in need. Finally, a special thanks to Brad Clark for coming up with the name Barley, so fitting, so perfect, so him! He IS Barley, the possum!

— Lea Murray

Barley's team that has helped him in many ways include, from left, Jade Sceusa, Dr. Linda Register, Brad Clark, Lea Murray, Gail Diederich, and Dr. Michele Farrar.

Introduction

This is the fascinating story of Barley Murray, a domesticated possum*, and his unique and special relationship with his human mama.

There is limited public knowledge about possums, and, often when encountered, they are approached with caution followed by a hasty retreat. For many, a possum does not, at first, appear to be an attractive or engaging animal.

Possums, like all wild animals, have a place in the natural order of things. Their environment, in most cases, is the wild. Barley, however, has enjoyed a much more interesting lifestyle.

The relationship of Barley and Lea Murray developed in an unusual way. Random circumstances brought them together. Lea, a registered veterinary technician, was working the night shift at an emergency specialty animal hospital when a woman arrived with a possum family that had been struck by a car. Lea's kind and gentle nature, coupled with her veterinary skills of more than a dozen years, and her lifetime love of animals sparked a desire to give a tiny vulnerable possum - the only one surviving - a chance to live.

It was Lea's desire to return the possum, once healthy enough, back into the wild where he would live in his native environment. Although improved, side effects from his injuries dictated he could not survive if released.

Lea worked with veterinarians, Florida Fish and Wildlife Conservation Commission, and the United State Department of Agriculture to obtain proper permits and licensing that allow her to legally care for Barley's lifelong needs. Along the way, Lea has chosen to educate people by offering information about possums and introducing them to Barley who has become the possum ambassador.

The international impact Barley has had could never have been predicted. Lea had no clue how her extraordinary relationship would develop with her special little pal.

Lea and Barley have become dedicated to building awareness about possums so they are realized as the unique and precious creatures they truly are. These efforts are evidenced by Barley's nearly 1,500 Facebook friends.

Barley's calm demeanor, agreeable personality, and his remarkable photogenic face are appealing, causing many people in public places to abruptly stop and say, "Is THAT a possum?! Wow! He's amazing!"

Lea has given Barley a "voice" and through it he has positively influenced people's impressions of possums and touched the hearts of countless individuals worldwide.

It is extremely important to emphasize that a possum is NOT a pet and no attempts should be made to capture a wild possum and try to turn it into a house pet.

*The pronunciation of "possum" for "opossum" is an example of aphesis where a weakly stressed vowel at the beginning of a word is dropped. This is especially noted in the American southern dialect as noted in the Merriam Webster dictionary.

In this story the word "possum" is used.

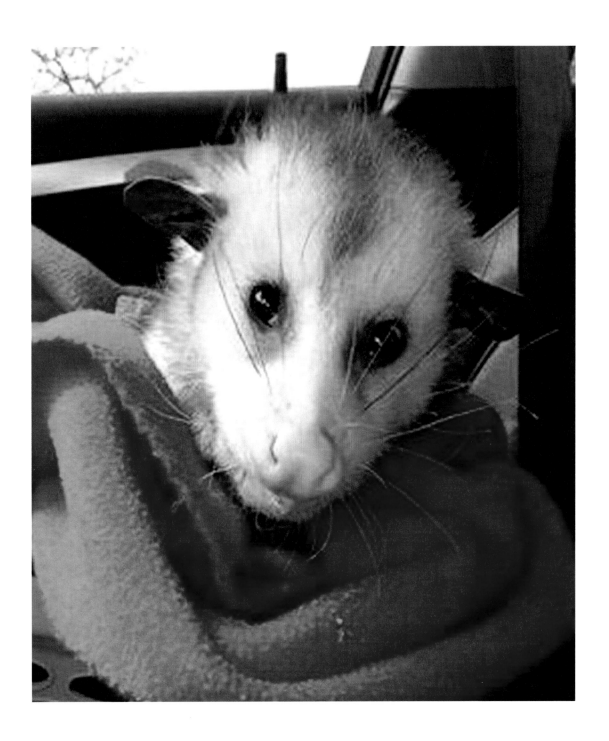

Hi! I'm Barley Murray. Yep! I'm a possum, and this is my story. My human mama, Lea Murray, helps me tell my story from the time she rescued me. I just celebrated my second birthday, and I'm a Tampa, Florida native.

There are many of my possum family members living mostly in the wild in the eastern United States. They wander in search of food and are often seen near garbage cans and roads.

I live a very different kind of life because of something that happened when I was very young.

FACT: The possum, specifically the Virginia possum, is North America's only marsupial. The female possum has a pouch, called a marsupium, where the babies live after they are born until they are old enough to survive on their own. Fossils of possums show they were on earth during the time of the dinosaurs.

I was a very small baby, about five weeks old, riding with my brothers and sisters on our mama's back. We were too big for her pouch and clung to her fur as she looked for food.

It was night, and our mama was too close to the road. A car hit us. We tried to hang on. A lady stopped, picked us up, and raced us to BluePearl Veterinary Partners Specialty and Emergency Hospital* in Tampa, Florida. I was the sole survivor. My leg was hurt pretty badly in the accident.

The first thing my human mama said about me was, "I want to give him a chance to live. I'll take him."

*BluePearl is one of nine nationally recognized veterinary trauma centers in the United States.

FACT: Possums are nocturnal. They wander at night in search of food. Possums do not see well. When they are near the road, car lights stun them and they freeze. When walking, possums move very slowly. They are solitary animals meaning they are usually seen alone.

Mama and the doctors took care of my leg. I still have a scar I show everyone.

Mama thought when I was healed I could go back to the woods and live in the wild like other possums. This is called "rehabilitate and release."

FACT: When wild animals are injured and need care, it is usually the goal to help them recover and return them back to their natural environment where they live with other animals of their own kind. This is often done successfully.

I was very tiny. At first, Mama fed me a special formula for possums through a tiny tube. She has lots of training in her veterinary work, but she had to hunt for the best ways to feed and take care of me. I was an orphan possum, and I really needed her help.

Soon, I was eating on my own, and I thought Mama was pretty special. I would crawl to her shoulders, get under her hair, and hang onto it just like I had done with my possum mama in the wild.

FACT: Female possums usually have five to eight babies in a litter. They are about the size of bumblebees when they are first born. They are born before they are ready to survive outside the female's body. They crawl to her pouch where they nurse and grow for two to three months. Then, the babies crawl out and hang on her back for another month or two.

I was a very interesting looking baby. My little nose was shiny and pink, and my little ears stuck out on both sides. They were almost transparent on the edges. Closer to my head, they were a darker solid color.

Mama learned my leg would never be completely right. I would always walk with a swagger. It's a funny walk and my leg works okay but not for climbing trees. Mama sometimes sets me in a tree, so I know what that feels like, but I can't do this alone.

Since I could not climb and take care of myself, I would stay with Mama for the rest of my life. I needed a name. Mama had two cats, and their names were Chowder and Porridge. Another soup name would be good. Mama liked "Barley". Sometimes she calls me "Bar-Bar". I like it when she calls me that!

FACT: Possums are excellent tree climbers and spend much time high in trees.

For me to stay with Mama, she had to get a permit from the Florida Fish and Wildlife Conservation Commission. Mama also had to learn about my diet and how to take care of me, so I stayed in good health. Mama also worked at East West Animal Hospital in Lutz, Florida. That's where my doctor, Linda Register, is a veterinarian. I love her very much. Together, she and Mama learned the best ways to help me.

FACT: Possums are omnivores. That means they eat both meat and plants. In the wild, possums eat insects, bugs and even snakes. They will also eat fruit that has dropped from trees. Because possums make the most of whatever food is available, they are called "opportunists".

I began to grow and get much stronger. Mama says she loves me more than anything in the world. I love her too. She said she'd always had pets and loved animals, but I was the best animal she'd ever had. I love to be hugged and I snuggle close to Mama.

I learned to go "potty" outside except in bad weather. Then, I use a "potty" pad indoors. I tell Mama when I need to go by pushing her with my nose. Mama says I'm smart and a fast learner.

FACT: Possums are wild animals and not considered pets. People are highly discouraged from trying to capture a wild possum and turn it into a pet.

Mama fixed a way to take me everywhere she goes. My travel buggy is actually a cat carrier she made into a comfy bed. Since Mama works in a veterinary hospital, my going with her is easy. I love to ride in the car, and I am strapped in, so I am safe. Mama and I spend as much time together as possible.

FACT: Possums have an average life span of two to three years in the wild. One possum in captivity lived for seven years.

I enjoy walking outdoors. I keep my nose to the ground and sniff things. My sense of smell is better than my vision. One day, when we were walking, two squirrels in a tree saw me and got pretty upset. They made all kinds of funny noises. I don't think they knew I can't climb trees, but I do like nuts, and I would have loved it if they'd dropped me one.

I walk slowly and don't see the need to hurry for anything. When I am ready, I can go back inside. Sometimes, Mama carries me. She stays near and I do not wander around alone.

FACT: Possums clean up road kill and this is why they are often seen near roads.

On our walks, we always find interesting places. This gives me experiences like I would have if I were a wild possum. I enjoy smelling different plants and flowers. Sometimes, I even get into the dirt. I wander without paying attention to where I am. Mama is never far away. She looks out for me.

FACT: Possums have a body temperature that is believed to be too low to incubate the rabies virus. If a pet, such as cat or dog, is bitten by a wild possum they should see a vet for a tetanus shot to prevent infection from bacteria, but rabies is not a main concern.

My tail is very unusual. Many possums have a skinny tail, but mine is thick and looks sort of like a rope. It has scales and tiny white hairs on it. I use my tail to help me balance. Often when I am sleepy, I will curl up and hold onto my tail

FACT: Possums have a long tail that appears bare but actually has tiny hairs on it. A possum's tail is muscular and is used for gripping. Possums do not hang upside down by their tails. In most cases, their tails would not support their body weight. Baby possums do use their tails to hang on when they are riding on their mother's back before they are old enough to walk alone.

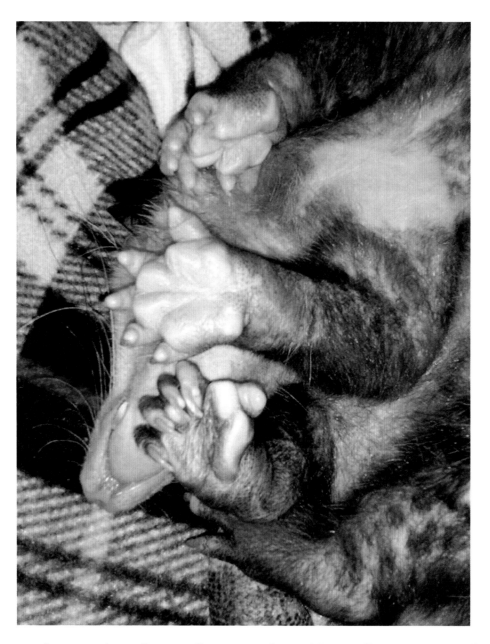

My feet are interesting. On my front two feet, I have five digits or "fingers".
On my back two feet, I also have five digits or "fingers", but one of them
on each foot is an "opposable" digit like a human thumb. It helps me to
hold onto things. I do not have nails on my "thumbs" like humans do. My
feet are very soft and shiny because Mama keeps me very clean.

FACT: Possums have very sharp claws on all four feet. The claws help with gathering food and tearing it apart to make it easier to eat. The claws also help in climbing trees.

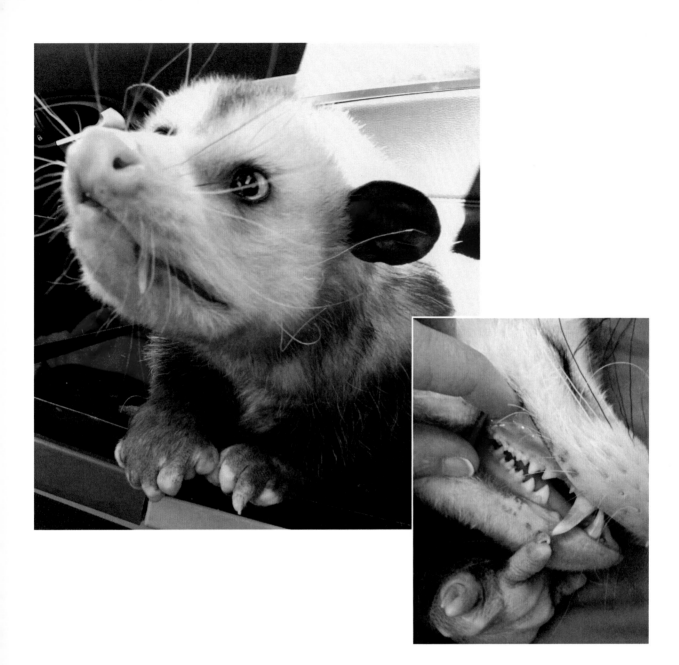

I have plenty of teeth including two very long canines on either side of my mouth. I am very gentle, and I do not bite anything except my food. I love to eat good things and stay healthy. I love vanilla cream filled cookies, but I don't get those often. Mama says they will make me gain too much weight.

FACT: Possums have 50 very sharp teeth. That's more teeth than any other mammal has. When they are scared, wild possums curl their lips, bare their teeth, hiss, and growl. They look quite frightening, but this is their defense.

I love all kinds of good food. I'm pretty lucky to get shrimp to eat and I even eat the tails because they are good for me. I like cheese and I love cheese pizza, but I don't get these often. I like yogurt and cottage cheese. Once, Mama threw away my empty cottage cheese carton after I'd eaten all of it. I went to the trash can and found the empty carton.

"Oh Bar-Bar, you're pretending to be possum!" Mama said. Then, she laughed and hugged me.

FACT: Possums in the wild will often wander close to houses and raid trash cans. They will also eat pet food if it is left outside.

I really love fruits, especially grapes. I take a grape in my mouth, and use my teeth to turn the grape around and around. I get the skin off. Then, I eat the juicy inside, and I spit out the grape skin.

FACT: In Florida, possums will eat citrus fruit like oranges that have fallen from the trees. In northern climate, possums enjoy eating wild persimmons.

I love all kinds of vegetables especially steamed broccoli and Brussels sprouts. Sometimes, I use my little "hand" to help get the food in my mouth. If I get messy, Mama has a way to take care of that.

FACT: Broccoli and Brussels sprouts are packed with vitamins and are good for possums and people.

When Mama thinks I need it, she gives me a bath. I am not crazy about this. In this picture, I had grabbed my towel and pulled it into the sink with me. Things were really a mess, and I was STILL in the water and soap.

This is my pouty face. Mama blow dries me. As you can see, I am not crazy about this either. The dryer makes me all fluffy, and my hair gets fuzzy.

FACT: Possums have a reputation for having a foul smell. In the wild, this may be from eating carrion (road kill) or being around rotting fruits and vegetables.

After I get a bath, I like to snuggle up with my soft toys and take a long nap. This is what I do most of the time. I love to nap.

FACT: Possums sleep most of the day. They roam at night and hunt for food.

Mama made a cozy place for me to be safe and snug when we go places. I have all my blankets and my cuddly animal friends with me. I have stuffed possums that look just like me. I like my blankets, and I can crawl under them. Sometimes, I use my tail to pull the blankets around me.

FACT: In the wild, possums often sleep in trees. Sometimes, they will find a hollow tree and sleep there.

I have many favorite places and ways to sleep. I enjoy a nice "human" bed with comfortable pillows and warm blankets. My very most favorite place is lying right next to Mama.

FACT: When possums have grown accustomed to living with humans, they often adapt their schedules to more closely resemble human patterns of being awake and being asleep.

I go to work with Mama. I have a bed behind the reception desk. I know where it is, and I can sleep there all I want. Sometimes, it looks like I am spilling out of my bed. I am SO comfortable.

FACT: When wild possums are frightened, they often will fall down and appear to be lifeless. This behavior has created the term "playing possum" which is a defense mechanism when an animal seems to be dead.

In February 2013, we celebrated my first birthday at East West Animal Hospital. Over 200 people came. There were t-shirts that said, "I partied with Barley the possum". They were sold to raise money that was donated to help save and care for other wild animals. I felt very happy about that.

In April 2013, a story in the *Tampa Bay Times* told about Mama and me and how I was rescued after the accident. People really like the story. We were invited to be on television, and that was pretty exciting!

Mama set up a Facebook page for me. People from around the world wanted to be my "friend". They were eager to learn more about me. Mama helped me post pictures and tell about my life. Pretty soon, I had over 1,500 Facebook friends.

During the Christmas 2013 season, we had a "Very Barley Christmas Party" at East West Animal Hospital. There was a photo booth where people could stand beside me for a picture. A lady made jewelry and Christmas ornaments with my picture on them. They were sold, and money from the party was donated to wildlife rescue *again*. It was a great party.

I was invited to enter an online "cutest pet" contest. Mama sent in this picture. Thanks to all my Facebook friends who voted for me, I won the contest and was on the cover of a calendar for January 2014.

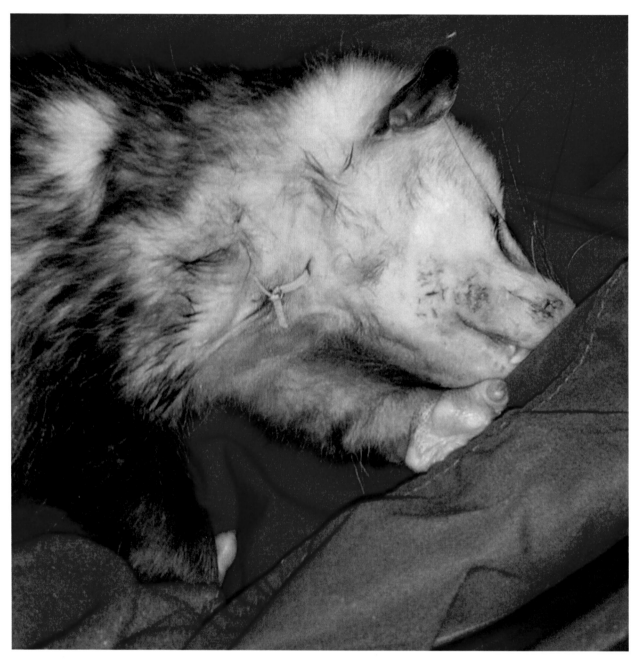

Possums often get idiopathic abscesses. I got them on my neck and face. Dr. Michele Farrar performed surgery to drain them and clear up the infection. I was pretty miserable for a short time. Mama took really good care of me. I'm glad she is a vet tech and knows what to do to help me get better quickly.

FACT: An idiopathic abscess is a very bad sore without a known cause. It is not clearly understood why possums get them easily.

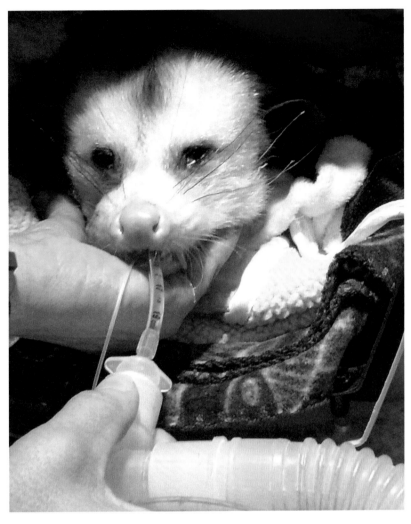

I snuggled with Mama while I got better. Mama worries about me when I have surgery or when I am sick. She's doing everything she can for me to live a long and healthy life.

I recovered very quickly. I got fruit treats that I love very much. I got Brussels sprouts and yogurt too. Mama makes sure I eat healthy foods that are good for possums.

FACT: Adult possums usually weigh about 12 pounds with males weighing a bit more than females.

I turned two years old, and there was another party. I got two bowls of steamed broccoli and loved it. Many people came to see me. I got lots of presents. Mama says I am one spoiled possum.

Mama read my birthday cards to me. I got up close and stared at them. I see things better at a short distance. Not many opossums get to have birthday celebrations. I am very lucky to have many friends and to be loved by so many people. I think I have the best friends in the whole world.

From my story, I hope people will understand possums better. When people see possums by the road, I want them to slow down and try very hard not to hit the possums. I hope by learning about me people will understand all wildlife better. All of us have a special place in this world.

I thank my human mama, Lea Murray, for loving me and taking care of me. I have gotten to live a really good life because she cared enough to give a hurt little baby possum a chance to live.

Love to everyone who has learned from my story, is my friend, and cares about possums.

Barley Murray

Glossary

Words are in order of their appearance in the text.

Marsupial – an animal that has a pouch where their babies grow after birth until they are completely developed

Nocturnal – active during dark hours

Solitary – alone, not in groups

Rehabilitate – to restore to good health

Release – let go

Orphan – having no parents

Litter – a group of young such as a litter of baby animals

Swagger – a swaying walk

Prehensile – gripping

Permit – a certificate or document allowing someone to do something specific

Omnivore – eating both plants and meats

Transparent – thin, allowing light to pass through

Life Span – number of years of life

Opposable – a thumb that can be placed against other digits or fingers for holding or grasping things.

Idiopathic – of unknown origin or cause

Carrion – road kill

Abscess – a small sore like spot that is filled with pus and shows infection is present

Extended Instructional Suggestions

1) Think about what you thought or knew about a possum BEFORE you read this book and think about and discuss ways your thinking has changed AFTER hearing this story.

2) Create a shoebox diorama or create a poster of a habitat where Barley would live in the wild.

3) Using a T-chart for Barley's living environment and a wild possum's environment show what is the same and what is different for the two.

4) Choose another animal similar to Barley such as a raccoon and compare and contrast the two.

5) Create a timeline of events in Barley's life.

6) Discuss and list some of the problems Barley has dealt with and how they are managed or have been overcome.

7) From Barley's pictures in this book, list words that describe him.

8) Discuss the kind of person Lea is and choose words that describe her relationship with Barley.

9) Discuss the ways Lea could properly take care of Barley in comparison to someone else. What skills or knowledge did she have that others might not have?

10) How has Barley helped other animals and how can you help animals?

11) Draw a chart showing cause and effect of events in Barley's life.

12) Discuss and list the steps of what to do if you see a wild animal hurt.

Resources

National Opossum Society
P.O. Box 21197
Catonsville, Maryland 21228
www.opossum.org

Dr. Linda Register, DVM
East West Animal Hospital
1524 Land O'Lakes Blvd.,
Suite 101
Lutz, Florida 33549
www.eastwestanimalhospital.com

Opossum Society of the United States
P.O. Box 16724
Irvine, CA 92623
www.opossumsocietyus.org

CONTACTS:

Gail Diederich: g.diederich@verizon.net

Barley Murray: www.facebook.com/barley.murray

Gail Diederich, a Franklin, North Carolina native, is a retired reading specialist and a 10 year staff writer for the *Tampa Bay Times*. She lives in Tampa, Florida, with her husband, Jay, and much loved beagle, Eddie.

Lea Murray, a native of Massena, New York, received her A.A.S. degree in Veterinary Technology and has worked as a Registered Veterinary Technician and Practice Manager for 18 years. She holds great compassion for all animals, especially her three cats and "the love of her life", Barley the possum.

Photo Credits

Cover photo: Michelle Devlin
Acknowledgements page photo by Keth Luke
Photos from the collections of Lea Murray, from Gail Diederich
and from Barley Murray Facebook via contributions of Barley's friends.

CPSIA information can be obtained
at www.ICGtesting.com
Printed in the USA
LVXC02n2229280714
396468LV00001B/1